The
GIVING BOOK

Open the Door to a Lifetime of Giving

by Ellen Sabin

and _____

WRITE YOUR NAME HERE

WATERING CAN® PRESS
www.wateringcanpress.com

WATERING CAN®

Growing Kids with Character

When you care about things and nurture them,
they will grow healthy, strong, and happy, and in turn,
they will make the world a better place.

All Watering Can Press titles are available at special quantity discounts for bulk purchases for sales promotion, premiums, fund-raising, educational, or institutional use.

Watering Can Press offers customized versions of this book and will adjust content for use by nonprofits and corporations in support of their community outreach and marketing goals.

To inquire about bulk discounts or to learn more about customized book runs, please visit our Web site or e-mail info@wateringcanpress.com.

Text and illustrations © 2004 by Ellen Sabin

WATERING CAN is a registered trademark of Ellen Sabin.
Watering Can, New York, NY
Printed in China in May 2012

Written by Ellen Sabin
Illustrated by Kerren Barbas
Designed by Heather Zschock

ISBN: 978-0-9759868-0-6

Web site address: www.wateringcanpress.com

Dear _____,

Because you are such a nice, wonderful, kind, and caring person, I am giving you this **GIVING BOOK**.

When you use it, you will be making the world a better place, making many people happy and healthy, and making me very proud of you.

You can use this book to help so many people because you—and your actions—are powerful. You make a **BIG** difference because you are so special.

From, _____

Before we get started, since this is
about giving and being thankful,
here are some "thank you's" of my own:

To my parents, for teaching me charity and love.

To Leah, who inspired me to write the first draft of this book
for her sixth birthday and who has taught me so much
as I watch her use it, use it, and use it....

To the angels—some tried and true—like my sisters, Debby and Elissa;
and others who seemed to pop out of nowhere to inspire, edit, cheerlead,
and otherwise help create this book (and teach me about giving) in
countless ways: Marc, Peter, Rick, Courtney, Alan, Karin, and Carra.

This book—and every giving act it may, perhaps, inspire—
is dedicated to my Nanny, who I love with all my heart.♥

A NOTE TO PARENTS
Our mission: To make the world more beautiful—one child at a time.

We know that once children learn about giving and charity:
they'll see how rewarding it is;
they'll learn how connected we all are;
they'll learn how powerful and significant they can be, and
they will, in turn, nurture the world around them.

This book will inspire them.

It will also create a keepsake of their wishes, dreams, hopes, and actions.
This activity book will become the scrapbook to their lifetime of giving.

Imagine your six-year-old giving $3 to feed someone who's hungry;
participating in a walk-a-thon at age ten; spearheading a charity drive as a teenager.
How cool will it be to have a record of their giving? Wow!
Now that would be one incredible and beautiful story of their life!

Table of Contents

What is The **GIVING BOOK?**

Welcome to Your
GIVING BOOK!

Think about someone who has helped you
or given you something special.

- Maybe you needed help with your homework and a teacher, friend, or someone in your family helped you.

- Maybe someone gave you a gift that you really needed or wanted.

- Maybe someone cheered you up when you were sad.

Isn't it a great feeling when someone helps you
or gives you something you need?

Well, YOU can help other people feel special, too!

YOU can make them happier.
YOU can make them healthier.
YOU can make the world a better place.

This book will help you do just that!

What are you waiting for?
Turn the page and get started!

How does **THE GIVING BOOK** work?

First You think about your hopes and wishes for making other people happy and healthy and for making the world a better place.

Next You decide the things you want to do to make those hopes and wishes come true. Your actions are valuable and powerful and can make a difference!

Then You get to DO THINGS—all sorts of things—to help others. You can give to people you know or to people you've never met. You can even do things to help the planet or animals.

And You get to do this OVER and OVER and OVER again, as much as you like, for as many different people and in as many different places as you want!

It's that easy!

REMEMBER: This is YOUR book. Along the way, you can keep a journal, draw pictures, send notes, and collect ideas about all of the ways you have given, you will give, or you want to give to others.

What are GIVING and CHARITY?

GIVING and CHARITY are when you see someone or something that needs help, support, or love and you decide that it matters to you to help so you jump in and do something.

- **Sometimes** we see or hear about people who need help and we feel sad for them because we want them to be healthy, strong, and safe. If someone is sick and you visit that person or send a card, that's GIVING and CHARITY.

- **Sometimes** we realize that we can do things to help solve problems like litter and pollution. If you help pick up trash in your neighborhood, that's GIVING and CHARITY.

- **Sometimes** we can join a bigger group and work with other people to help solve big problems. If you work with your church, synagogue, or school to help others, that's GIVING and CHARITY.

When you wish to make the world better and then you do something to make that wish come true, that's GIVING and CHARITY!

Whether it's something kind and giving you do to help your parents, friends, neighbors, or even people who live far away;

Whether it's giving away some of your time, money, toys, artwork, or simply your kindness and love;

GIVING and CHARITY are what connect us all and make the world a better place!

And you make a
BIG DIFFERENCE
in the world!

Write down your VERY OWN definition of **GIVING** and **CHARITY**.

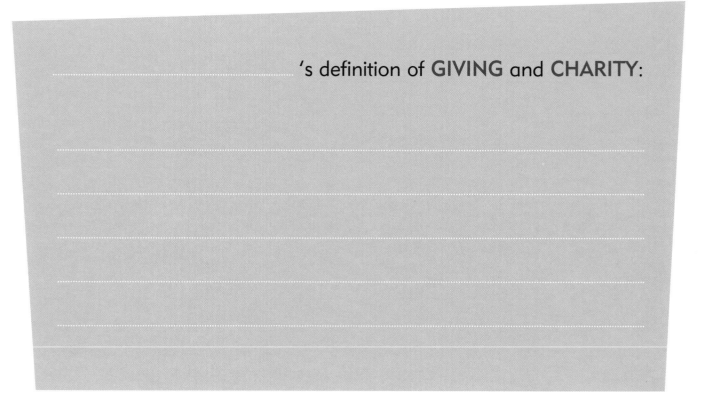

....'s definition of GIVING and CHARITY:

Now, let's see what other people are saying about **GIVING** and **CHARITY**.

Ask someone in your family, your babysitter, or teacher how THEY
would define these words. Write their definition below.

My Favorite GIVING Fable!

There was a boy walking down a deserted beach just before dawn. In the distance, he saw an old man who was picking up stranded starfish and throwing them back into the ocean.

The boy watched in wonder as the old man again and again threw the small starfish from the sand to the water.

He asked, "Old man, why do you spend so much energy doing what seems to be a waste of time?" The old man explained that the stranded starfish would die if left in the morning sun.

"But there must be thousands of beaches and millions of starfish!" exclaimed the boy. "How can you make any difference?"

The old man looked down at the starfish in his hand, and as he threw it to the safety of the ocean, he said,

"I MAKE A DIFFERENCE TO THIS ONE."

(This story was adapted from a poem by Randy Poole titled, "The Difference He Made.")

Your actions make a difference.

YOU can help so many people
in so many ways!

Who's been GIVING to YOU?

Can you think of people who have been giving to you or have shown you acts of charity? List things people have done to help you or to make you feel special.

Who shared with you?

_____

What did he or she share?

_____

_____

_____

Who taught you something?

_____

What did he or she teach you?

_____

_____

_____

Who showed you love?

_____

How did he or she show you love?

_____

_____

Who made you happy?

_____

How did he or she make you happy?

_____

_____

Doesn't it make you feel great when people are giving to you?

How have YOU been GIVING?

What have you done that was giving to other people? List ways you've shown kindness or helped people.

Who have you shared with?

_____

What did you share?

_____

_____

_____

Who have you taught?

_____

What did you teach them?

_____

_____

_____

Who did you show love to?

_____

How did you show your love?

_____

_____

_____

Who have you made happy?

_____

How did you make them happy?

_____

_____

_____

Don't you feel great about yourself when you give to others?

for Others and the World Around You

Maybe you want to help make the world more peaceful.

Maybe you want to help people who are sick.

Maybe you wish the world were cleaner and less polluted.

Maybe you think everyone should get a chance to learn how to read and write.

Maybe you want to help people who don't have homes.

Maybe you hope to help people who can't see or walk or who have other special needs.

Maybe you want to help people who live in countries far, far away who need food or medicine.

What are you THANKFUL for?

List the things that you are thankful to have.

1. .... date: ....

2. .... date: ....

3. .... date: ....

4. .... date: ....

5. .... date: ....

6. .... date: ....

7. .... date: ....

8. .... date: ....

More things that you are thankful to have in your life.

9. .... date: ....

10. .... date: ....

11. .... date: ....

12. .... date: ....

Now that you've listed things that you're thankful for, turn the page and think about what you wish for other people.

Wishes for **OTHER PEOPLE** and the **WORLD**

List the things that you wish everyone in the world could have and the things that you think would make the world a better place.

1. .... date: ....

2. .... date: ....

3. .... date: ....

4. .... date: ....

More Wishes for Others...

5. .... date: ....

6. .... date: ....

7. .... date: ....

8. .... date: ....

9. .... date: ....

10. .... date: ....

11. .... date: ....

12. .... date: ....

Now, let's see how you can make those wishes and dreams come true!

Your ACTIONS make a BIG difference

Kind and Caring Things You Can Do to be Giving to Others

What You Do Can Help People in Many Ways!

Your wishes and dreams are probably pretty big, right?

Good, because every day there are things that you can do that are nice and caring and loving.

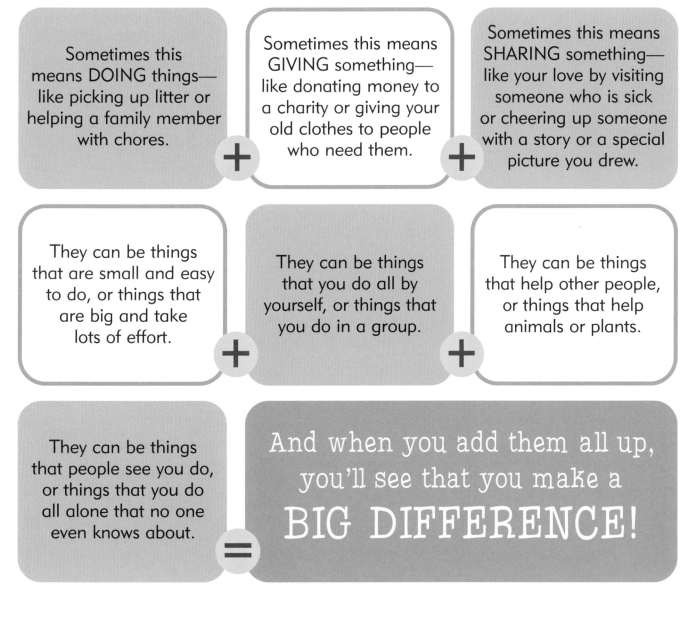

Sometimes this means DOING things—like picking up litter or helping a family member with chores.

+

Sometimes this means GIVING something—like donating money to a charity or giving your old clothes to people who need them.

+

Sometimes this means SHARING something—like your love by visiting someone who is sick or cheering up someone with a story or a special picture you drew.

They can be things that are small and easy to do, or things that are big and take lots of effort.

+

They can be things that you do all by yourself, or things that you do in a group.

+

They can be things that help other people, or things that help animals or plants.

They can be things that people see you do, or things that you do all alone that no one even knows about.

=

And when you add them all up, you'll see that you make a **BIG DIFFERENCE!**

What can YOU do?

Look at the pictures on this page. Each drawing shows a person who needs something. Next to each picture, write how you can help that person.

You and your ACTIONS have an effect on the world around you!

There are LOTS of things that you can do to make people happy, solve a problem, or do something nice for others. Here's a fun and easy one... and it even rhymes!

This poem describes a special gift that you can share. Can you guess what it is?

This is something you can give
To everyone you see
It's a gift so valuable
Although it's also free

It doesn't take a lot of work
You can't buy it in a store
You can give so many everyday
And you'll always still have more

All you do is lift your cheeks
And spread a little cheer
You can even show some teeth
To everyone who's near

Can you guess this special gift?
Think about it for a while
It's written right there on your face

Of course it is a ....!

Kind and caring things you can do to be **GIVING** to others

- You can help your family by offering to clean the house, play with your sister or brother, or take care of your pet.

- If you know someone who is lonely or sad, you can make them cookies and visit them so that they can have company and feel your love and care.

- If you wish the world were cleaner and less polluted, you can go outside with your parents or friends and pick up trash or help plant a garden.

- You can help people by teaching them things that you already know—like showing your little brother how to ride a bike, or helping a friend understand a homework assignment.

- There are groups in your area that help feed people who don't have food. You can ask a parent or friend to help you collect food and take it to one of these places.

What are your ideas for
ACTIONS and ACTIVITIES?

Write down things that you can do or ways that you can give your time, your love, or your care to other people to make them happier and healthier.

1. ....

2. ....

3. ....

4. ....

5. ....

6. ....

7. ....

8. ....

What's the **GIVING** story?

These drawings show people helping others and being giving. Can you come up with a story to go along with each picture? Then share your stories with a friend!

May I help you?

Read each fact below. Then read an idea about how **YOU CAN HELP**!

FACT 1: Every minute, an area of forest equal to twenty football fields is lost because people use SO MUCH paper.

To Help: Recycle! By recycling one ton of paper, you will save 17 trees. You should also reuse paper when you can. Spread the word and tell your friends and family members how important it is to recycle and reuse.

FACT 2: 70% of people in the world don't have clean water to drink. We all need to keep water clean and not waste it.

To Help: Turn off the water when you are not using it—like while you're brushing your teeth.

FACT 3: There's enough food in the world to feed everyone, but almost one billion people go hungry each day.

To Help: You and your friends can organize a talent show! You can dance, sing, put on a skit, play an instrument—whatever! Invite your family and friends to your event, and charge $1 for admission. Then donate the money you collect to a charity that helps feed hungry people.

What are some of the SPECIAL THINGS that you can do?

We all have special skills and talents that make us unique.
Another way to be GIVING is to share your skills and talents with others.
People always like it when you share with them.

- If you are a good singer, you can visit someone who needs cheering-up and sing to them.

- If you can read well, you can read to someone who can't read. You can even help someone learn how to read.

- You can put together a skit or a play for people and bring some sunshine into their day.

- If you know a lot about something—like a different language, a subject at school, or a game—then you can teach others about it. Teaching is a great way to share a part of yourself.

- Maybe you're strong and can help your neighbors shovel the snow if they look tired.

- You can draw pictures or make art to give to someone. People love handmade gifts!

There are so many ways that you—and all your special talents—can help other people EVERY DAY!

List some of your special **SKILLS** and **TALENTS** that you can share with others:

The World Around You

You've seen how you can be thoughtful, kind, caring, and GIVING to other people. You can also be gentle and GIVING to nature and the world around you.

Animals, forests, rivers, flowers, and all living things need to be cared for and nurtured in order to grow and be healthy.

And there are tons of things that YOU can do to help THEM!

Draw a Picture

Draw a picture of YOU doing something special to help or protect nature.

WRITE YOUR NAME HERE

Makes the World a Better Place!

Every time you do something giving and kind for other people or for the planet, write about it here. You can write about when you help people, when you share, and all the other things you do that make a difference in the world!

Date:

Who you helped and how:

Date:

Who you helped and how:

Date:

Who you helped and how:

Date:

Who you helped and how:

Date:

Who you helped and how:

Date:

Who you helped and how:

Date:

Who you helped and how:

Date:

Who you helped and how:

Helping Others by Donating Your
MONEY or THINGS

You have learned how you can help others with your time,
your kindness, and your talents. Another way to help others is
to give, or donate, your money or things to charity.

● Find a bag or box around your house. This will be a special kind of piggybank.
We will call it:

's GIVING BAG.

_____

WRITE YOUR NAME HERE

● You can decorate your **GIVING BAG** in all
sorts of fun ways to make it special and
unique.

● Then, save money in your special **GIVING
BAG**. When it's full, you'll decide where you
want to send that money to help make your
wishes and dreams for people and the world
come true.

● You can save money again and again and do
this over and over and over—as much as you
like—for as many different people or places
that you want!

Your money, your decisions...and YOU!

Whenever you get money—maybe for a birthday present or an allowance or for doing a chore—you should always think about what YOU want to do with the money.

You may want to SPEND some of it on something you want.

You may want to SAVE some of it to buy or to do something special later.

You can also start saving some money to GIVE to charity. This is the money you'll put in your GIVING BAG.

Then, decide what you want to do with your GIVING BAG money. Think about your wishes and dreams for making the world a better place.

- There are people who need food or clothing so they can be healthy and happy.

- There are doctors and scientists who need money to help sick people or to find cures for diseases.

- You can give money to help save animals or protect the environment.

There are so many different ideas!

Once you decide who YOU want to help with your money, ask someone—a parent, teacher, or friend— to help you figure out where to send your money to make your wishes come true.

How much can you save?

Here's a calendar page so that you can keep track of how much money is in your **GIVING BAG**. First, fill in the dates. Then, whenever you put money in your **GIVING BAG**, write on the calendar how much you've put in. At the end of the month, add it up.

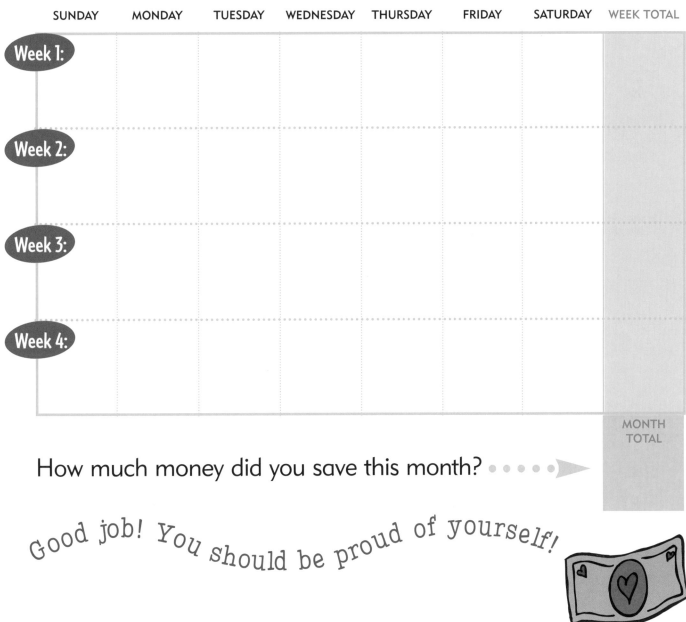

	SUNDAY	MONDAY	TUESDAY	WEDNESDAY	THURSDAY	FRIDAY	SATURDAY	WEEK TOTAL
Week 1:								
Week 2:								
Week 3:								
Week 4:								
								MONTH TOTAL

How much money did you save this month? ● ● ● ● ● ▶

Good job! You should be proud of yourself!

Send a letter with your money

When you're ready to send your money to help other people, here's what you can do:

● Talk to someone in your family and choose a charity to help.

● Then decide the best way to send your money.

● Write a letter to send with your money. In your letter, you can write about yourself and why you like to help other people. Here's an example of a letter you can send to the charity:

> Dear ....,
>
> Hi! My name is ....
>
> I am .... years old.
>
> I want to help people feel safe, healthy, and happy. I also want to help make the world a better place.
>
> Here is some of my money that I saved to help others.
>
> I think that you do good work helping others and I want to help, too.
>
> From, ...

Draw a Picture

Draw a picture of some of the people or things you have helped by donating your money.

THE GIVING BAG

Makes the World a Better Place!

You can keep track of all the good things you do with the money you give!
Every time you donate your money to help people, list it here.

Date: ....

Who you helped :

....

Why you made that choice:

....

....

....

Date: ....

Who you helped :

....

Why you made that choice:

....

....

....

Date: ....

Who you helped: ....

Why you made that choice: ....

....

Date: ....

Who you helped: ....

Why you made that choice: ....

....

Date: ....

Who you helped : ....

....

Why you made that choice:

....

....

....

Date: ....

Who you helped : ....

....

Why you made that choice:

....

....

....

Date: ....

Who you helped: ....

Why you made that choice: ....

....

Want to give EVEN MORE?

Money is not the only thing you own that can help others. Sometimes we have things—old things, new things—that would be nice to share or give away to other people who might need them.

Here are some other ways to be giving:

- Collect all the clothes that you've outgrown. Clean them, fold them, put them in a box, and bring them to the Salvation Army, Goodwill, the Red Cross, or another donation center that will give your old clothes to people who need them.

- Every once in awhile, take one of your old toys—or even one of your new toys or presents—and give it to a child who doesn't have toys.

- You can even organize your family to go through the house to collect things that you might want to give away to other people.

- Sometimes schools or churches have food drives to collect canned goods to feed people who are hungry. Ask a parent if you have extra food in your cabinets that you could give to people who need food to be healthy.

- You can collect the books you don't read anymore and donate them to your local library so that other people can enjoy reading them.

Fill in the blanks

Can you and your family finish these sentences about giving?

In the kitchen, we can find some .... and send it to people who are hungry.

In the winter when it gets cold, it's nice to have a warm .... to wear outside.
Maybe we have some clean, used ones that we can donate to people.

It's fun and important to know how to read. In our house, we have a lot of ....
that we can give to others so that they can enjoy reading, too.

For my birthday, I get a lot of .... Maybe I can give one of them
to a child who doesn't have what I have so that they can play, too.

Other things around the house that might be nice to give to other people who
need them are:

....

....

....

....

....

....

GROUP
ACTIVITIES

Fun Ways for You and Your Friends to Make the World a Better Place

If one person can do so many things to help others, a group of people can do even more!

Here are some group activities that you can organize to do EVEN MORE GOOD and SHARE THE FUN OF GIVING.

- You and your friends can go to a park with trash bags and clean up all the litter.

- Have all of your GIVING BOOK friends put their GIVING BAG money together and decide as a group how you will use it to help others. That's a lot of money to share with people who need it!

- You and your friends can get together and make all sorts of cool art projects— drawings, paintings, and other crafts. Then you can use those projects to do good in your community. You can set up a stand to sell the art, then donate the money you collect to charity.

- Have a grown-up help you and your friends bake cookies or treats and take them to a hospital, elderly home, or anyplace that people can use some love and cheering up!

We Can Count on You!

How much of a difference does your giving make in the world? Chances are, it's a **HUGE DIFFERENCE**—and there's no stopping you! Here's a great way to see just how much good you and your friends are doing.

First, find a large jar. Then, keep your eyes open for change. Each time you, a family member, or a GIVING BOOK friend or classmate has "spare change," that person can add their penny, nickel, or dime to the jar. You'll be surprised at how quickly it adds up!

When the jar is filled, have everyone guess how much money has been collected. The person who comes closest can decide what to do with the money. They may choose to give it to a favorite charity, buy food for a soup kitchen, or even donate it to a library, animal shelter, or toy drive.

What a great way for your giving to go on, and on, and on!

Keep an Eye on Your Wishes

Sometimes it helps to make your wishes and dreams come true by writing them down and keeping an eye on them!

Here's a group art project idea. Get together with your friends or classmates and create a "Wishes for the World" wall. Here's how:

3. Hang your stars—your dreams and wishes—on the wall at your home, school, or wherever.

1. Take several big pieces of paper and cut them into the shape of stars.

2. On each star, write your wishes about making other people happy and healthy and the world more wonderful.

Then you can see everyone's kind wishes on the wall and be one step closer to making them come true!

EXPRESS Yourself

How Does Being GIVING Make You Feel?

's

WRITE YOUR NAME HERE

THOUGHTS and FEELINGS

When I give to others, I feel...

EXPRESS YOURSELF

Your Very Own
GIVING JOURNAL and SCRAPBOOK

We're leaving the next couple of pages blank for you.

Here's why: We know we didn't think of everything. You probably have other **GREAT FUN** ideas about how to use these pages!

You can:

Fill these pages with photos of the people you've helped!

Write your own GIVING fable!

Fill these pages with drawings and pictures about giving and charity!

There are so many great ideas for using these pages!

OTHER STUFF

YAY YOU!

Congratulations! You've done so many kind and caring things. This GIVING BOOK certificate shows that you know how to give the best of yourself to others and the world.

#1

THE GIVING BOOK

This certificate is awarded to

....
WRITE YOUR NAME HERE

for being kind and giving to others and the world.

....
DATE

Now that you know how great it feels to help make the world a better place, get out there and tell your friends and family how important it is to give. The more people there are who learn about charity, the better our world will be.

Thanks to Others

Wherever your travels may take you, you're sure to meet people who are kind to you. How can you thank them? In their own language, of course!

Here's a list of how to say "thank you" in different languages. How many can you learn?

Language	"Thank you"	Pronunciation
Afrikaans	Dankie	(dahn-key)
Chinese	Xie xie	(syeh syeh)
French	Merci	(mare-see)
German	Danke	(dahn-kah)
Hawaiian	Mahalo	(ma-hahlo)
Hebrew	Toda	(toh-dah)
Hindi	Sukria	(shoo-kree-a)
Indonesian	Termi kasih	(t'ree-ma kas-seh)
Italian	Grazie	(gra-see)
Japanese	Arigato	(ahree-gah-tow)
Portuguese	Obrigado	(oh-bree-gah-doh)
Russian	Spasibo	(spah-see-boh)
Spanish	Gracias	(gra-see-us)
Swahili	Asante	(ah-sahn-the)
Swedish	Tack	(tahk)

Family Talk

Here are some quotes from famous folks about **GIVING** and **CHARITY**. Perhaps they will spark a great family conversation about giving, charity, or the famous givers who said these words.

"It's not how much we give, but how much love we put into giving."
—Mother Theresa

"I don't know what your destiny may be, but I think I do know that the only ones among you who will be truly happy are those who have sought and found a way to serve."
—Albert Schwietzer

"If you want happiness for an hour, take a nap. If you want happiness for a day, go fishing. If you want happiness for a lifetime, help somebody."
—Chinese proverb

"Try to make at least one person happy every day. If you cannot do a kind deed, speak a kind word. If you cannot speak a kind word, think a kind thought. Count up, if you can, the treasure of happiness that you would dispense in a week, in a year, in a lifetime."
—Lawrence Lovasik

And, especially for the adults out there...

Of all the dear sights in the world,
Nothing is so beautiful as a child
When it is giving something.
Any small thing it gives.
A child gives the world to you.
It opens the world to you as if it
were a book
You'd never been able to read.
But when a gift must be found,
It is always some absurd little thing,
Passed on crooked...
An angel looking like a clown.
A child has so little that it can give,
Because it never knows
It has given you everything.

—Margaret Lee Runbeck

Reference Ideas for Adults

Kids may need a parent, family member, or teacher to help them research how they can make their wishes and dreams for a better world come true.

To research more about non-profit organizations and charitable causes, you can check your local phone book, go to the library, or inquire at your church, synagogue, mosque, or community center. Or you can look on the many websites that provide both general information with listings of charities, as well as organization-specific information about a particular charity.

Below is a brief list of some general charity-related websites.

Guide Star
Information on non-profit organizations
www.guidestar.org

National Charities Information Bureau
www.give.org

Charity Navigator
A non-profit organization dedicated to
helping givers make intelligent decisions
www.charitynavigator.org

Kids Care Clubs
www.kidscare.org

Join Watering Can® Press in growing kids with character.

www.wateringcanpress.com

- See other Watering Can® series books.
- Order books for yourself or to donate to an organization of your choice.
- Take advantage of bulk discounts for schools and organizations.
- Learn about customizing our books for corporate and community outreach.
- View the FREE Teacher's Guides and Parent's Guides available on our site.

We hope that all of your
WISHES and **DREAMS**
for helping people
come true!